D0574530

HOW CAN I EXPERIMENT WITH ... ?

GRAVITY

Cindy Devine Dalton

Cindy Devine Dalton graduated from Ball State University, Indiana,
with a Bachelor of Science degree in Health Science.
For several years she taught medical science in grades 9-12.

Teresa and Ed Sikora

Teresa Sikora teaches 4th grade math and science. She graduated with a
Bachelor of Science in Elementary Education and recently attained National Certification
for Middle Childhood Generalist. She is married with two children.
Ed Sikora is an Aerospace Engineer, working on the Space Shuttle Main Engines.
He earned a Bachelors of Science degree in Aerospace Engineering from the
University of Florida and a Masters Degree in Computer Science from the
Florida Institute of Technology.

Rourke Publishing LLC
Vero Beach, Florida 32964

PROJECT EDITORS
Teresa and Ed Sikora

PHOTO CREDITS
Gibbons Photography
NASA
Walt Burkett, Photographer

ILLUSTRATIONS:
Kathleen Carreiro

EDITORIAL SERVICES
Pamela Schroeder

Library of Congress Cataloging-in-Publication Data

Dalton, Cindy Devine, 1964–
    Gravity / Cindy Devine Dalton.
        p. cm. — (How can I experiment with?)
    Includes bibliographical references and index
    ISBN 1-58952-013-0
    1. Gravitation—Juvenile literature. 2. Gravitation—Experiments—Juvenile literature [1. Gravity.
    2. Gravity—Experiments. 3. Experiments.] I.Title

QC178.D35 2001
531.14'078—dc21   00-066530

Printed in the USA

Gravity: The natural force that causes objects to move toward the center of Earth.

Quote:

"If I have seen further than others, it is by standing upon the shoulders of giants."

-Isaac Newton

Table of Contents

What Does Gravity Look Like?

Can you see gravity? Yes, in a way you can. You can see that objects always fall down—never up! This seems normal to us. But what if you lived in outer space? Objects wouldn't fall down. They would float. Why? Outer space has a lot less gravity than we have on Earth. Gravity is not a thing, like a ball or a person, that we can see. However, we can see the effects of gravity. This is called **gravitational force**.

Imagine jumping up and floating! Thanks to gravity we always come right back down to the ground.

What Is Gravity?

In this book, we are going to think about gravity on Earth.

Gravity is the **attraction** between objects. The bigger the objects are, the bigger the gravitational force will be. The Earth, being so big, has a very strong gravitational pull. Gravity always pulls toward the center of the Earth. It keeps us walking on the ground instead of in the air.

As you begin learning more about **physical science**, you will see that many sciences have laws. Laws are rules to follow that get an end result. The law of gravity is a very important law of science.

Since the Earth is so big, it has a very strong gravitational pull toward its center.

GRAVITY

GRAVITY

GRAVITY

GRAVITY

Mass and Distance Affect Gravity

The force of gravity depends on the **mass** of objects and the **distance** between them. Here on Earth the gravity is pulling on all objects equally. That means if you were to stand on a chair and drop an apple and a grape they would hit the ground at pretty much the same time. Because the apple and grape are not too far away from Earth, gravity affects them equally. However, when things are great distances away, like the moon and stars, the mass and distance affects gravitational pull.

Objects like bubbles do not have much mass. They are affected by air resistance more than the gravitational pull. So they float.

Look at the night sky. The stars you see are suns very much like our own sun. We are so far away from them we are not affected by their gravitational pull. The Earth is 93 million miles (150 million km) away from the sun. Even though that is a great distance, the sun is so massive that it has enough gravitational pull to keep the Earth orbiting around it! Wow! Distance and mass do affect gravitational pull.

What Is the Law of Gravity?

The law of gravity says that the gravitational force between the two objects depends on the mass of the two objects and the distance between them. The bigger the mass of a planet, the more gravitational force it will have. For example, the Earth's gravity is 6 times greater than the moon's because the Earth has more mass. That's why it is easier for the astronauts to jump around on the moon. They don't have much gravity pulling on them. The farther apart two objects are, the less gravitational force there is between them.

Did you know that the law of gravity is what keeps the moon in orbit around the Earth and the Earth in orbit around the sun?

Remember the stars that are so far away from us? They're massive, but because we are so far away we don't feel any gravitational pull toward them. Gravity is a force that pulls objects toward each other even when the objects are not in contact with each other. Gravity is the "glue" that holds our universe together.

Where Is Gravity?

Gravity is almost everywhere, even in space. The gravitational force of the Earth keeps the Space Shuttle in orbit around it. Astronauts float inside the Shuttle. They are being pulled back to Earth by gravity with exactly the same force as the **centrifugal force** that is pushing them away from Earth. Centrifugal force is the force we feel pulling outward when you spin an object around at the end of a string—like a yo-yo when you do "around the world". A great place to feel centrifugal force is at the fair. Find a ride that spins you around really fast. You will notice that you are being pulled outward from the center of the spin. That is centrifugal force.

The International Space Station, like the Space Shuttle and its astronauts, is affected by gravitational and centrifugal force.

Centrifugal Force

Gravitational Pull

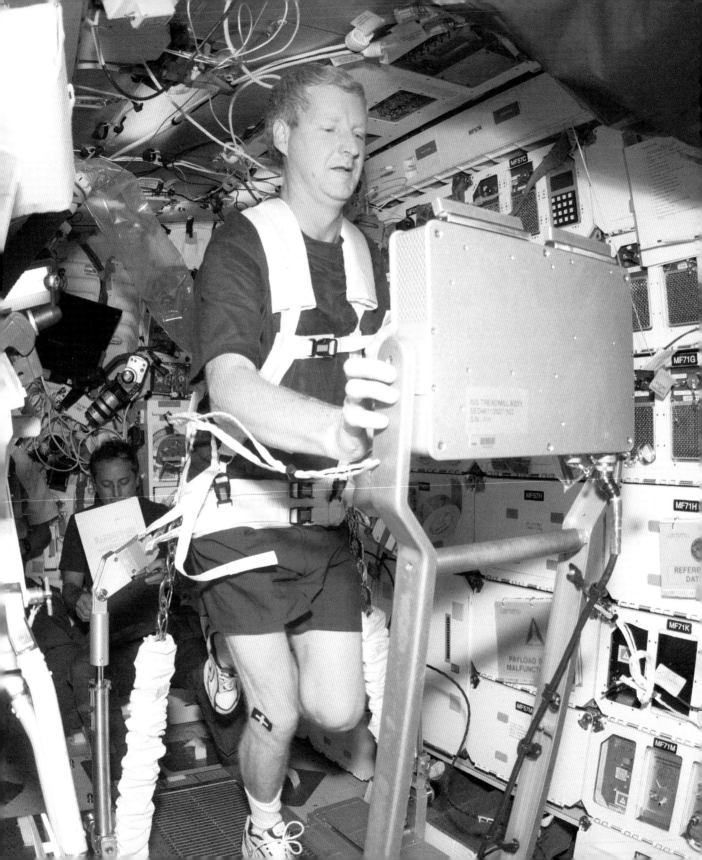

Does Gravity Make Us Strong?

Yes, gravity helps us to be strong. An example is in our bones. Bones need to be strong so that they do not break easily. If we exercise a lot, lift heavy objects, or push and pull things around, our bones get stronger.

In space, our bones do not stay as strong because they are not pushing or pulling anything. Astronauts must exercise in space to keep their bones and muscles healthy. Floating around all the time does not work their bones. If you were in space for a long time, your bones would become weaker than they are on Earth.

This astronaut is trying out a new piece of exercise equipment that will help him stay healthy in space.

Could We Get Sick in Space?

Yes, we could. Gravity affects our balance. Our ears contain fluid that makes our bodies stay in balance. When our bodies are out of balance, we feel **motion sickness**. Have you spun around in circles and then had a hard time standing up straight? That is being out of balance! These things won't hurt us, but they do change our health.

Getting off of a spinning swing can make you feel sick. Motion sickness makes your stomach upset because your ear canal's fluids are not in balance.

Out of This World Questions

Question:

How do astronauts sleep in space?

Answer:

Like babies. That is, astronauts sleep all wrapped up and strapped to the wall—or the ceiling if they like! Astronauts tuck their arms into a pouch so they won't float. How would you like to be awakened by a floating arm during the night?

Question:

How do you go to the bathroom in space?

Answer:

Since there is no "drainage" in space, spacecraft toilets are more like vacuum cleaners. They suck the waste into a container where it is dried and pressed together to save space. Wastewater is put out into space. Scientists are now studying a way to recycle the waste for use while in space.

Question:

Could I save enough of my allowance to buy a space station?

Answer:

Only if you earn about $25 million a week and save for a whole year! So far, the International Space Station has cost $13 billion.

Question:

Since water floats in space, how do astronauts take showers?

Answer:

Astronauts take sponge baths! It would be very hard trying to get soap off while floating with the water!

Isaac Newton and Albert Einstein

Do you wonder why things fall down? Do you wonder why things fall at the same speed, or with different force? That is what Mr. Isaac Newton did—and he figured it out. Isaac Newton was an English mathematician who saw an apple fall from a tree.

Instead of "falling," he thought of it as being pulled to the ground. That is where his research began.

Albert Einstein was also a famous mathematician who studied gravity. However, he felt that Isaac Newton was not quite right in his ideas about gravity. Albert Einstein produced the theory that improved on Newton's. Einstein was a very intelligent man who focused on the study of physics. Physics is the study of heat, light, motion, sound, and matter. There were many men in history who studied physics, but these two are the most famous!

Sir Isaac Newton

Do You Get Shorter During the Day Because Gravity Is Pulling You Down?

What you need:

- Tape
- Pencil
- Book or ruler
- Piece of paper

Try This:

1. Before you go to bed at night, tape a piece of paper on the wall at the level of your head, and a little higher. Label one side morning and one side night. Lay a book beside the wall.

2. As soon as you wake up in the morning stand right in front of the paper and place the book on your head.

(You should be leaning against the wall.) Make a mark on the paper showing how tall you are.

3. Before you go to bed at night, measure yourself again. Put the book back on your head, and make a new mark. Did you shrink?

4. When you wake up in the morning, measure again. You will probably be the same height (maybe even taller if you grew) as you were yesterday morning!

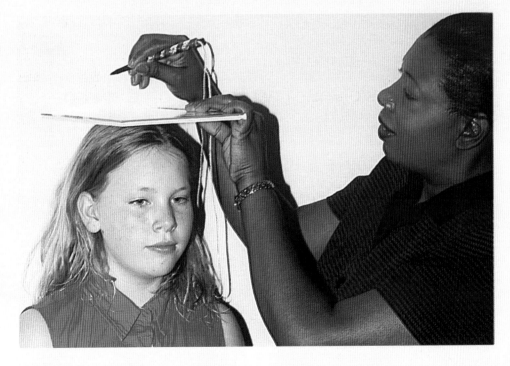

A Way to Show the Gravitational Force Theory

What you need:

- Newspaper
- 2 apples
- 1 grape
- A partner

Try This:

1. Place newspapers on the floor.
2. Stand while your partner lies on the floor looking at the newspaper.
3. Hold an apple in each hand. Extend your arms straight out away from your body (over the newspaper) so that each apple is the same height from the floor.

4. Let go of both apples at the same time. Did they hit the newspaper at about the same time?
5. Now stand in the same position but this time hold an apple in one hand and a grape (or some other small object) in the other hand. Let go of both objects at the same time. Do they land at the same time, too?

What Happened?

Notice how the apple and grape hit the floor at the same time. Most people would have guessed that the apple would hit the floor first. We know that gravity pulls all objects downward at the same speed, no matter how much they weigh.

It is important to measure carefully in every experiment.

Glossary

attraction (eh TRAK shen) — a force that brings things together

centrifugal force (sen TRIF yeh gel FORS) — a force that pulls objects outward when they are spun around quickly

distance (DIS tens) — the amount of space between two objects

gravitational force (grav eh TAY shen el FORS) — the force that draws things together

mass (MAS) — how much matter is in something

motion sickness (MO shen SIK nes) — being sick to your stomach because you're moving

physical science (FIZ ih kel SY ens) — science that deals with nonliving things

Further reading

International Space Station: A Journey Into Space
International Space Station: A Space Mission

Websites to visit

www.spartechsoftware.com/reeko
www.spacekids.com
www.kennedyspacecenter.com
  (click on just for kids)

Index